CUT ENERGY CORDS OF ATTACHMENT

Book 3 in the series: LifePurpose©

Marleene Stuart

LifePurpose©

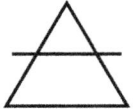

Copyright © 2022 Marleene Stuart

All rights reserved

The characters and events portrayed in this book are fictitious. Any similarity to real persons, living or dead, is coincidental and not intended by the author.

No part of this book may be reproduced, or stored in a retrieval system, or transmitted in any form or by any means, electronic, mechanical, photocopying, recording, or otherwise, without express written permission of the publisher.

ISBN-13: 9798802427194

Cover design by: Marleene Stuart
Library of Congress Control Number: 2018675309
Printed in the United States of America

*...to picking up a handful
of red sand in the Sahara desert
and feeling it run through my fingers...*

CONTENTS

Title Page
Copyright
Dedication
Introduction
Preface
Cut Energy Cords Of Attachment   1
1   3
2   8
3   11
4   13
5   16
6   19
Epilogue   33
Afterword   35
About The Author   37
Books In This Series   39
Books By This Author   41

INTRODUCTION

Quantum physics teaches that your thoughts and words create your reality...

Just like everything around you, your words have a specific vibration...

When you criticize yourself, your negative self-talk triggers symptoms of stress - irritability, frustration, forgetfulness, lack of focus, emotional exhaustion, anger, anxiety, depression, burnout...

Your mind causes vibrations that are continually at work. Your feelings and thoughts all have a frequency. A thought is a frequency just like light, sound, ultra-violet or radio waves. Your thoughts vibrate constantly through your mind and whether you're aware of it or not, your thinking manifests in your environment and your reality.

When you choose different thoughts and words, you choose to create a different reality...

In every relationship that you have, you are exchanging energy with the other person. This exchange of energy exists in the form of cords that you use to connect with others.

This energy can become a negative energy cord or a positive energy cord.

Negative energy cords can shift energy into life destructive behaviour patterns like fear, distrust, doubt, obsession, jealousy or resentment. They can also cause you to take on emotional problems that belong to others. This can have the effect that you feel stuck and are unable to move on when you need to or want to.

When you choose to cut negative cords, you choose to create a different reality for yourself…

Positive energy cords can infuse your energy with courage, fortitude, respect, appreciation, excitement, gratitude and power. When you are connected to like-minded people, activities, passions or adventures, the positive energy exchange supports the expansion of your mindset.

PREFACE

you're in the right place at the right time...

if this is a difficult time in your life...

if this is a time of challenges...

or a time of transformation...

the words in this book are here to offer
you healing and blessings...

CUT ENERGY CORDS OF ATTACHMENT

MARLEENE STUART

Book 3

In the series: Life Purpose

1

*How to release negative
energy bonds*

As we move through our lives we grow, we learn and we evolve. From time to time we have to let go of that which no longer serves us. The process of letting go creates space. This space welcomes the arrival of new life, potential, and new possibilities.

Entrepreneurs seem to have always followed this mantra…

In the world around you, entrepreneurs are the best examples of individuals who follow 'learn, unlearn and relearn'. They are the restless lot, always passionate about their idea. They follow their commitment to reach their goals without respite. They learn from every mistake and do not hesitate to cut ties with something that is not serving their growth. They keep going in the face of obstacles. They explore the unknowns. They are willing to pivot their business model, to continue to build a successful business.

I recognise the following negative energy bonds in my life:

_____

_____

_____

_____

_____

_____

_____

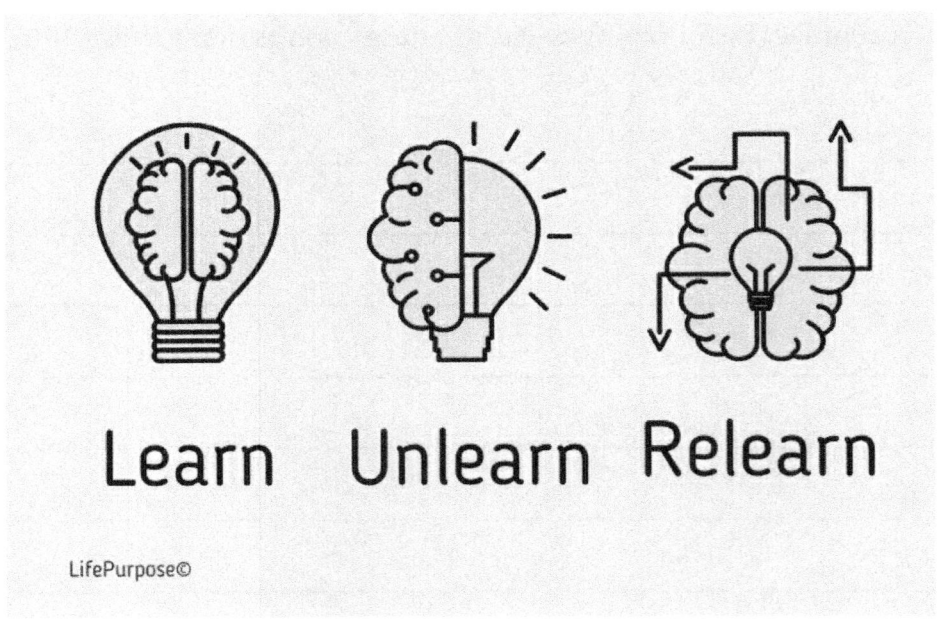

Cord-cutting is a very ancient and common practice in both secular and spiritual traditions. The practice of cutting cords helps to recover energy that has been lost or taken from you. It is also a great way to re-establish healthy energy boundaries in your life.

Let's explore the practice of cutting energy cords...

I recognise the following negative thinking patterns or behaviour patterns that don't serve me anymore:

_____

_____

_____

_____

_____

_____

_____

_____

2

*Cutting Energy Cords For
Creating New Space*

We develop energy cords when we enter into relationships with others. And this is true whether it is with an individual that you meet in passing, someone you have regular interaction with, a colleague, friend, family or an intimate partner. Energetic cords like aren't necessarily bad. They help us to understand each other and form long-lasting connections with one another.

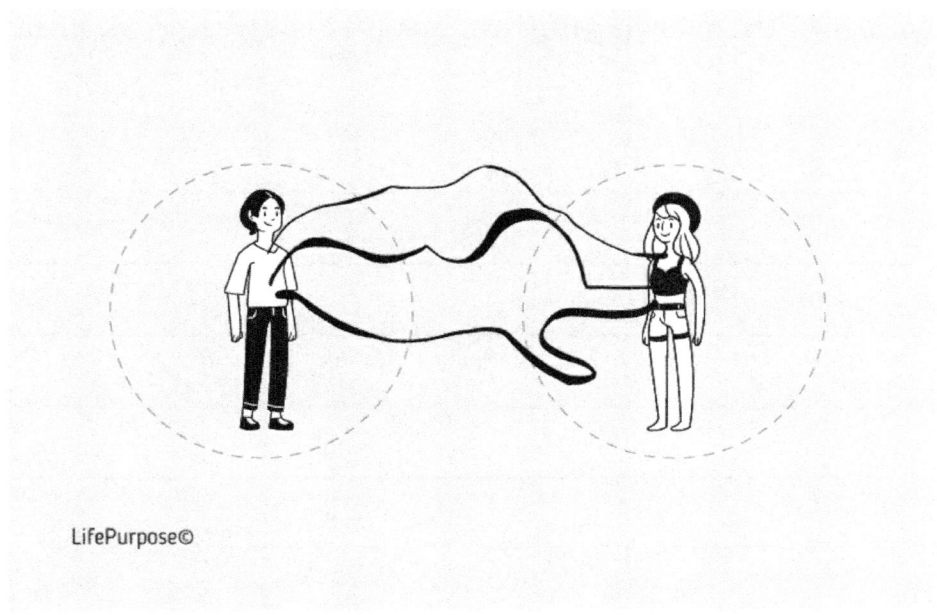

When we are connected energetically to others, we perceive information on a much deeper level. All of us can tune into the energy of another. While we mostly interact with our five physical senses, we also have intuitive ways of relating to the world. You've had the experience where you entered a room and became aware of the feeling that something unpleasant like an argument or anger had just taken place.

The truth is that energy is our primary means of relating. We are all energy beings. From time to time it is necessary to let go of these negative bonds to create space for new possibilities.

I recognise the following negative energy bonds with people in my life:

_____

_____

_____

_____

_____

_____

_____

3

Make A Transition By Letting Go

Every day we develop beyond what we were yesterday. If you were to continue accumulating all of the leftovers from past experiences, you would be weighed down by the heavy burden of it all.

Holding on to what was prevents you from moving forward. Right now, you can make a small step of transition by deciding to let go of something that is holding you back.

When you let go of what is no longer helpful, you can transition from one way of being to another.

This may mean that you do this while you are in a relationship with another person or it may simply mean changing the way you relate to life. It is always necessary to let go of what is no longer helpful to you.

While we are in relationships with others, we often tend to hold onto much more than is healthy for us. This "holding on" is unhealthy for all your bodies - physical emotional, mental and spiritual... in short, carrying all this redundant energy is unhealthy for your energy field...

When you cut energy cords you let go of the burden of the past. This transition frees your senses and enables you to move forward feeling lighter with a sense of willingness and appreciation for new possibilities.

I am letting go of the following negative energy bonds with a situation/job/event/house/dream:

_____

_____

_____

_____

_____

_____

_____

4

An Energy Deficit

Often we maintain these energy cords long after a relationship has ended. They can be very subtle such that we are not even aware that they're there. However, you might already be aware that an accumulation of cords from many people has the effect of a slow depletion of your energy. This will create an energy deficit in your energy field.

"It is not the strongest of the species that survives, nor the most intelligent that survives. It is the one that is the most adaptable to change."
~ Charles Darwin

CHANGE

LifePurpose©

Change is the only constant. You arrived on this page because you understand that learning is essential for anyone who wants to develop as well as thrive in the world we live in today.

The following situations deplete my energy:

_____

_____

_____

_____

_____

_____

_____

5

Signs Of Negative Unhealthy Cords

- Feelings of unexplained sadness, lethargy, depression
- Depleted energy levels
- Obsessive thinking about others
- Often speaking about others in a deprecating or judgmental way
- Unable to make decisions or feeling 'stuck'
- Getting sick often, lowered immune system function
- Addictive behaviour – seeking comfort in excesses such as drinking, binge eating, drugs, smoking, as well as excessive over-exercising or workaholic behaviour.

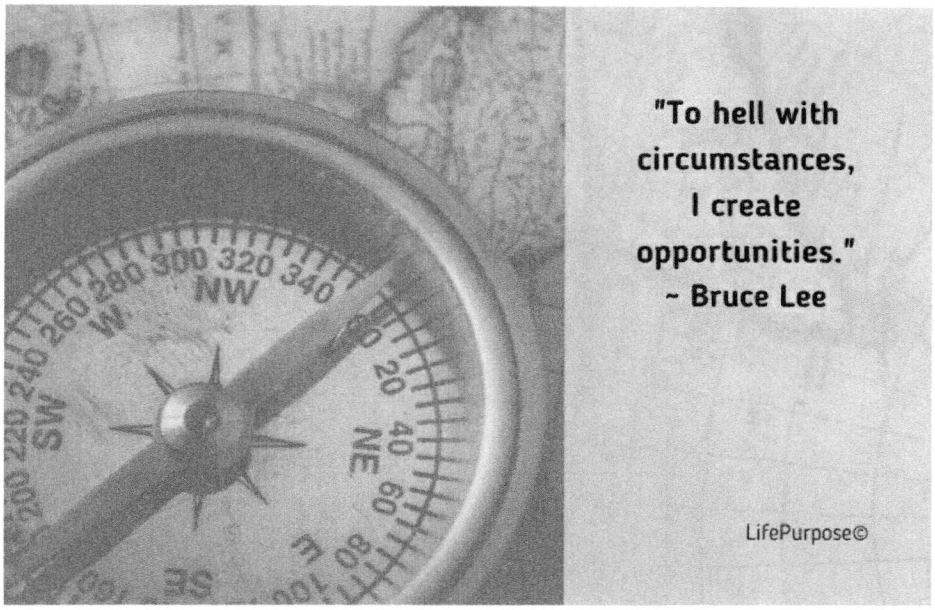

"To hell with circumstances, I create opportunities."
~ Bruce Lee

LifePurpose©

It may seem that this quote has a tone of irritation and resentment. However, it ends with an enthusiastic, confident resonance. You can choose to be the victim of circumstances. You can choose to create solutions.

Life is meant to be lived...

It is not enough to only think about things, to contemplate and mull over...

You are creating the energy that you are sending into your environment...

Find positive, life supportive solutions...

Up to now, I have maintained these unhealthy negative energy cords:

_____

_____

_____

_____

_____

_____

_____

6

Cord Cutting Rituals: How To Release Negative Energy Cords

Our culture celebrates mental and intellectual processes. "Thinking" your way through things to find solutions are the most suggested behaviour. However, to regain the energy that you have lost through negative cord connections, you must engage with your awareness of energy.

There are many ways to cut negative cords and establish healthy energy boundaries.

SALT BATH

SALT BATH

Add:
½ cup of Epsom salts to the water (you can also use a blend of Epsom salts and sea salt)
4-5 drops of organic lavender oil
Light candles & incense

LifePurpose©

As you soak in the warm water, set your intention. In your mind's eye, see all the negative energetic cords dissolving in the water. Inhale white light through the top of your head and feel it flow through your body, filling your arms and legs. Reclaim your energy and feel your energy filling your body and flowing to your arms and legs. Take note of the feeling of rejuvenation and being in a state of balance.

So it is. It is done.

My notes/understanding/intuition/insight/vision…

SMUDGING

SMUDGING
Pull back the twine that binds your bundle so it doesn't catch fire. Hold your sage bundle at a 45-degree angle and light it. After about 10 seconds, blow out the flame you created, and allow the embers to continue burning. The smoke will rise from the bundle and you can now waft the smoke through your home to clear all negativity from your surroundings.

LifePurpose©

During traditional indigenous ceremonies all over the world, the sacred smoke from medicinal or sacred plants is used to purify or bless people and places. Smudging is a ceremony to purify or cleanse the negative thoughts or soul of a person or place.

Say the following affirmation:

"I cut all negative energy cords of connection. I reclaim my energy now. All negative bonds are cleared from this space. This is my sacred space and this space supports my connection with the Divine/my higher self/soul/spirit/inner nature."

So it is. It is done.

My notes/understanding/intuition/insight/vision...

JOURNAL WRITING

JOURNALING
Write a letter to the other person.
Say everything that you have been wanting to say.
Don't hold back.
State your desires and your frustrations.
When you are done, burn the letter as a symbol of release.

LifePurpose©

Writing brings about the transformation of emotions and thoughts.

Say the following:

- I reclaim the energy that has been freed with the burning of this letter.
- Take a moment to feel your energy flow back into your body.
- Feel your energy field that is now filled with vitality and new possibilities.
- So it is. It is done.

My notes/understanding/intuition/insight/vision…

VISUALIZATION

VISUALISATION
Sit/lie down in an area where you will not be disturbed
In your mind's eye, see the person you wish to cut energy cords with
You can use a sword, a knife or scissors to cut the cords
In your mind's eye, see the energy cord that connects you
Become aware of where in your body you feel the cords
Now, place your intention on the cords, visualize yourself cutting the cords

LifePurpose©

Take the time to sit in an area where you will not be disturbed during your visualization. In your mind's eye, see the person you wish to cut energy cords with. You can use a sword, a knife or scissors to cut the cords. In your mind's eye, see the energetic cord that connects you with the other. Become aware of where in your body you feel the cords. Now, place your intention on the cords and visualize yourself cutting the cords between you.

Speak the following blessing:

- I sever all negative energy cords that do not serve my highest good.
- All negative energy cords are cut, across all dimensions, times and planes.
- Thank you for the role you played in my life.
- I release you from the effect of these negative bonds,

across all dimensions, times and planes.
- I reclaim my lost energy that has been freed with the cutting of these negative cords.
- Take a moment to feel your energy flow back into your body.
- Feel your energy field that is now filled with vitality and new possibilities.
- So it is. It is done.

Spend some time sitting in quiet meditation. Feel the vibrant energy of new possibilities in your energy field. Bring your awareness back to the present time. Step confidently forward into your day.

MARLEENE STUART

My notes/understanding/intuition/insight/vision...

"A man can achieve great things if he can conquer himself."
~ Bruce Lee

Feel Empowered...

I'm Sexy... What's Your Superpower...?

You Are A Radio Station

Do What You Love What You Do Journal

My Sexy Gratitude Notebooks #1 - 44

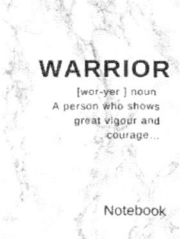

Warrior Notebook

I Am Editing My Life Journal

Send us your transformational stories, photos, & videos
lifepurposehq@gmail.com

VISIT OUR STORE
Feel Sexy, Free & Empowered...

EPILOGUE

I admire your courage during times of transformation... I respect the work that you do to clear barriers within yourself...

Once upon a time, I was in a group with Masaru Emoto while we said a blessing to water... I experienced the elevation of the vibration of the energy in me, in the people around me and in the environment as every single water molecule in every part of our bodies responded to the blessing of love and gratitude... In memory of this life-changing experience, I am saying this blessing to you today...

I love you, I thank you

I love you, I thank you

I love you, I thank you

Marleene Stuart

April 2022

AFTERWORD

Your Passion.

Your Life Purpose.

Our Purpose.

This book is part of the series: Life Purpose. Visit us to find more ways to clear the habits and behaviour patterns that don't serve you anymore. Feel empowered, free, and successful…

Find your Life Purpose…

ABOUT THE AUTHOR

Marleene Stuart

Marleene Stuart has lived in South Africa, Croatia, Cyprus and Shanghai, China...

At the moment, she lives in Africa next to the Indian ocean with a view of tropical plants while she sips her coffee...

When it gets quiet around her, you can always hear the whisper of adventure beckoning...

Somewhere in the cupboard under the stairs, she has two gold medals for gold panning...

BOOKS IN THIS SERIES

LifePurpose©

Feel empowered, appreciated and successful...

ELEVATE YOUR ENERGY: Understand how the energy of thoughts and words can elevate the frequency of energy within you and around you...

POWERFUL VIBRATION: This energy has the power to transform you, those whom you interact with, as well as the physical space that you occupy...

CREATE YOUR ENVIRONMENT: Find ways how you can use this information to create your environment and find your Life Purpose...

ATTRACT: Attract the experiences that are helpful to become the best version of yourself...
Feel empowered, appreciated and successful...

I'm Sexy... What's Your Superpower...?

Feel sexy, empowered & successful...

YOUR COMPANION: Your companion motivational guide, journal, planner, and notebook

FIND NEW WAYS OF BEING: Find ways to change your thinking from self-defeating to positive & self-enlightening.

INSPIRATION: Inspiration For Inner Strength & Self-Fulfilment. Find ways to take charge of your thoughts. Find words that put you ahead of life's challenges.

COME INTO ALIGNMENT WITH YOUR INNER NATURE: Find the secret to living a joyful life and connecting with your inner nature.

YOUR PERSONAL JOURNEY: You personalize this book of your life in the journaling space provided on each page…

You Are A Radio Station

Feel safe, successful & empowered…

FIND THE SECRET: Find ways to take charge of your thoughts. Find words that put you ahead of life's challenges. Find the secret to living a joyful life and connecting with your inner nature.

HOW TO MAKE YOUR BODY'S ENERGY SYSTEM WORK FOR YOU: You'll understand how your body's energy system works…

ATTRACT EXPERIENCES THAT ARE HELPFUL: Find ways to create your environment and find your Life Purpose… You'll know how to attract the experiences that are helpful to become the best version of yourself…

BOOKS BY THIS AUTHOR

My Sexy Gratitude Notebook

Feel sexy, empowered & successful…

YOUR SEXY JOURNAL: Notebook, planner, organizer, logbook… created for your daily enjoyment…

BEING YOURSELF IS SEXY: Find your favourites amongst the 44 titles and use them every day for your inspiration…

STEP INTO YOUR POWER: Appreciation, self-care, nurturing, gratitude & stepping into your own power is SEXY…

INSPIRATION: Inspiration & Personal Growth for entrepreneurs, leaders, influencers & empowered women everywhere…

Do What You Love What You Do

Feel safe, successful & empowered…

CREATED FOR YOU: A journal, notebook, composition book for your daily journaling and insights…

TAKE CHARGE OF YOUR MIND: Find ways to take charge of your thoughts. Find words that put you ahead of life's challenges.

CREATE YOUR ENIVIRONMENT: Find ways to create your environment and find your Life Purpose…

I Am Editing My Life

Feel safe, successful & empowered...

TAKE CHARGE OF YOUR MIND: Find ways to take charge of your thoughts. Find words that put you ahead of life's challenges.

CREATE YOUR ENVIRONMENT: Find positive ways to create your environment and find your Life Purpose...

INSPIRATION: Your companion notebook, planner, organizer, logbook, an inspirational journal for women, entrepreneurs, leaders, influencers & doers everywhere...

Chewing Gum Improves My Memory

Feel successful & empowered and proud of yourself...

INSPIRATION FOR YOU: A fun companion notebook, planner, organizer, logbook, and inspirational journal for women, entrepreneurs, leaders, influencers & doers everywhere...

TAKE CHARGE OF YOUR MIND: Find ways to take charge of your thoughts. Find words that put you ahead of life's challenges.

CREATE YOUR ENVIRONMENT: Find positive ways to create your environment and find your Life Purpose...

CHEWING GUM?: Yes, it works to improve your memory...

Cryptofolio Inheritance Journal

Feel validated, successful and proud of yourself...

Crypto Assets Inheritance Journal....

FOR YOUR CONVENIENCE: List your beneficiaries, cryptocurrency accounts, security keys and passwords...

IDEAL GIFT: Birthdays, Anniversaries, Graduation, Father's Day, Mother's Day, Any Day Gift...

You can take care of their future...

Printed in Great Britain
by Amazon